Farmyard Friends

Cows

Camilla de la Bédoyère

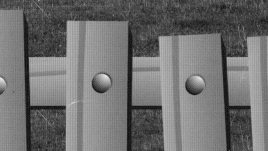

QEB

QEB Publishing

Editor: Eve Marleau
Designer: Melissa Alaverdy
Picture Researcher:
    Maria Joannou

Copyright © QEB Publishing, Inc. 2010

Published in the United States by
QEB Publishing, Inc.
3 Wrigley, Suite A
Irvine, CA 92618

www.qed-publishing.co.uk

Library of Congress Cataloging-in-Publication Data

De la Bédoyère, Camilla.
  Cows / Camilla de la Bédoyère.
    p. cm. -- (QEB farmyard friends)
  Includes index.
  ISBN 978-1-59566-940-7 (library binding)
 1. Dairy cattle--Juvenile literature. 2. Cows--Juvenile
literature. I. Title.
  SF208.D44 2011
  636.2--dc22

                        2010001130

Printed in China

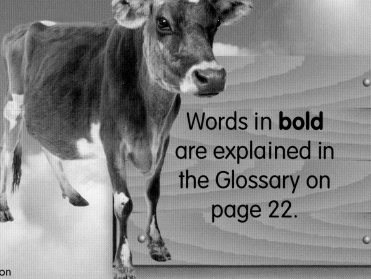

Words in **bold**
are explained in
the Glossary on
page 22.

Picture credits
(t=top, b=bottom, l=left, r=right, c=center,
fc=front cover)

Alamy Images Blickwinkel/Hecker 6t, Andrew Fox
12, Picture Contact/Ton Koene 13t, David R. Frazier
Photolibrary, Inc. 18–19, Grant Heilman Photography
20–21; **Corbis** Isabelle Vayron/Sygma 16, Alvis
Upitis/AgStock Images 19tl; **Istockphoto** Morganl
19tr; **Photolibrary** Imagebroker.net/Hartmut
Schmidt 8, Philip Quirk 11tr, Imagebroker.net/Michael
Krabs 12–13, Mark Hamblin 14l, EA. Janes 14r, All
Canada Photos/Ron Watts 14–15, Robert Harding
Travel/Mark Mawson 16–17, John Warburton-Lee
Photography 21t; **Shutterstock** Damian Palus cl,
Pichugin Dmitry cm, Kurt De Bruyn cr, Eric Isselée 2,
4l, Elenamiv 2–3, MisterElements 3, 5b, 7b, 9b, 11b, 13b,
15b, 17b, 19b, 20b, Aleks.K 4-5, Wikus Otto 5t, Sally
Wallis 6–7, Jean Morrison 7t, Nancy Gill 8–9, Laila
Kazakevica 9t, Nando Viciano 10–11, Mikhail
Malyshev 11tl, Jarno Gonzalez Zarraonandia 15t,
Svry 17t, Volker Rauch 18, Pixel Memoirs 20t, Kurt
De Bruyn 22, Nubephoto 24 (icons), Pichugin Dmitry
24 (background), Thomas M Perkins 24b.

Contents

What are cows?

Cows are large farm animals. They have hoofs on their feet with two toes.

head

Cows are mammals, which means they are covered in fur and feed their babies with milk. Milk is made in a special place on a cow's body, called an udder.

hoof

Cows and bulls are large animals with hooves and horns.

⬆ A hoof has two toes.

Cows have long tails with hair at the end. They flick their tails around to keep flies away. Some cows have horns on their heads. Bulls, or male cows, have the biggest horns.

horn

tail

udder

⇧ Cows and bulls can use their horns to attack other animals, or to fight each other.

Farmyard Fact!

Hoofs are hard and they protect an animal's feet. They are similar to your nails, which protect your fingertips and toes.

Cows on the Farm

Farmers keep cows for their milk and their meat. Cows live in groups called herds.

Thousands of years ago, cows were wild animals, but now they live on farms. Most cows are about 60 inches (1.5 meters) tall. That's the height of a small car.

⇦ Adult cows are large, strong animals.

Male cows are called bulls. Female cows are called cows. Young cows are called calves.

Cows are old enough to have calves when they are about two years old. ⇨

⬇ Cows and bulls spend most of their day lying on the grass.

calf

cow

Farmyard Fact!

Cows have very good eyesight. They can see in front, to the side, and even behind!

Where do cows live?

Cows that are kept for their milk are called dairy cows. They live on dairy farms.

Dairy cows spend most of their time in barns or in fields. If the cows spend the day in fields, they have shelters to keep out of the sun, rain, and wind. At night, they sleep in barns.

⬆ Shelters are safe, dry places where cows can rest.

Cows that live in barns are kept in **pens**. The floor is covered in sand or straw to keep the cows warm.

← Farmers clean the pens every day.

⬇ The fields where cows live are called **pastures**.

pen

barn

Farmyard Fact!

Cows sleep lying down. They only need to sleep for about four hours a night, but they sometimes nap during the day.

What do cows eat?

Cows are herbivores, which means they only eat plants. Farmers make sure their cows have plenty of food.

Most cows can **graze** on grass in the field, or they are fed **hay**.

On some farms, cows are also fed with grains, such as corn and barley. They may be given **vitamins**, too.

← A cow can spend seven hours a day grazing on grass.

Farmers put water troughs in the fields and barns. Then the cows can drink whenever they want to.

⬆ Cows eat from a food trough that is called a manger.

⬆ Every day, the farmer puts fresh water in the drinking trough.

Farmyard Fact!

Cows don't chew the grass very much before they swallow it. Later, the grass comes back into their mouth so they can chew it again! This is called "chewing the cud."

The daily life of a cow

Cows are also known as cattle. They spend most of their time feeding or resting.

Beef cattle spend the day grazing in fields.

Dairy cattle often live in **cowsheds** because they have to be milked every day.

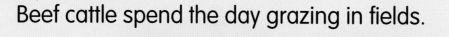

⇐ Dairy cows are kept in pens, ready for milking time.

Long-haired cattle ⇒ are kept outdoors to stay cool.

Farmers check their cattle to make sure they are healthy. They trim their cattle's hoofs to stop them getting too long and cracking.

⬇ Hoof trimming does not hurt cows. It helps keep their feet in good shape.

Farmyard Fact!

A dairy cow can drink more than 25 gallons (100 liters) of water every day. That's as much as a bathtub full of water!

The life cycle of a cow

Baby cows, or calves, grow inside their mothers. This time is called a pregnancy.

Calves are born in spring. The farmer helps a cow when it is time for her to give birth. Sometimes veterinarians are also needed.

⇧ When a calf is born, the mother licks it clean, and soon it can stand up.

⇐ Cows are pregnant for about nine months.

⬇ The calves move to barns or fields, and the life cycle begins again.

3

4

⬆ The calf drinks its mother's milk to grow strong and healthy.

Farmyard Fact!

Most cows give birth to just one calf at a time, but sometimes a cow has **twins**.

Beef cattle

Beef cattle are kept for their meat. They often live on big farms called ranches.

Farmers round up their beef cattle when it is time for them to go to **market**. The cattle will then be sold for food.

⟵ Ranch farmers often ride horses, and are called cowboys or cowgirls.

The meat from cattle will be sold for food. The skin of cattle is used to make leather.

The meat we get from ➪ cattle is called beef.

⬇ A farmer makes sure his herd is all healthy.

Farmyard Fact!

Shoes, bags, clothes, belts, and even furniture are often made of cow leather.

Dairy cattle

Farmers have to milk dairy cows at least once a day. A cow can make up to 5 gallons (20 liters) of milk each day.

The milk from dairy cattle is then **pasteurized** and sold in stores, or used to make other dairy products, such as cheese.

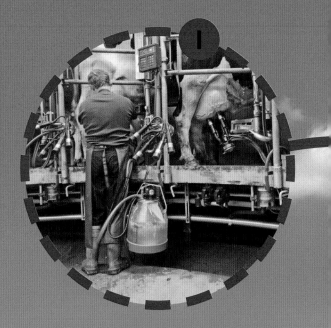

⇧ Milking machines take the milk from a cow's udder quickly and easily.

⇩ At the dairy, milk is pasteurized and put into bottles or cartons.

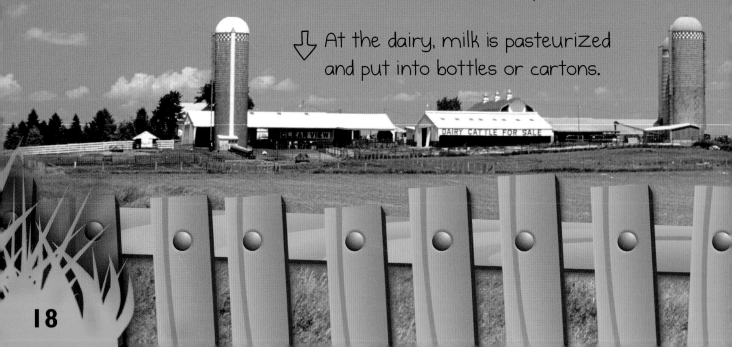

DAIRY CATTLE FOR SALE

↓ The milk is cooled down and put in a tanker.

3

2

⬆ It is then sold in stores and supermarkets. The milk can also be made into dairy products such as cheese.

Farmyard Fact!

When milk is pasteurized, it is heated to kill bacteria, or bugs, that might be living in it. It is then safe to drink.

Breeds of cattle

There are hundreds of different types of cattle. Each type is called a breed.

Some breeds are best for their milk, while others are best for their meat.

Many dairy farmers keep Holstein cows. Their fur is black and white, but no two cows have exactly the same pattern.

⬅ Holstein cows produce milk for about six years.

Holstein cow

Farmyard Fact!

Many foods contain milk. Ask an adult to help you look in your refrigerator to find some of them.

Ankole cattle live in Africa. They are kept for their milk, not for their meat.

Ankole cattle grow very ⇨ long, curved horns.

Herefords are large beef cattle. Farmers all over the world like to keep Herefords because they are very good for meat.

⇩ Hereford cattle have brown bodies and white faces.

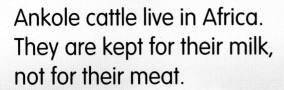
Ankole bull

Hereford cow

Glossary

Cattle
Cattle are animals with hoofs.
Cows and bulls are cattle.

Cowshed
This is a large farm building
where cows live or are milked.

Graze
Animals that feed on growing
grass are said to be grazing.

Hay
Grass that has been cut and
dried so it can be given to
animals to eat.

Market
This is a place where
farmers gather to
sell their animals.

Pasteurized
This means heating milk
to make it safe to drink.

Pasture
Land that is covered in grass,
where sheep and cows graze.

Pen
This is the small fenced
space where each cow
can stand or rest.

Twins
When a cow gives birth to two
calves at the same time, they
are called twins.

Vitamins
Food contains vitamins. They help
animals and people to grow and
stay healthy.

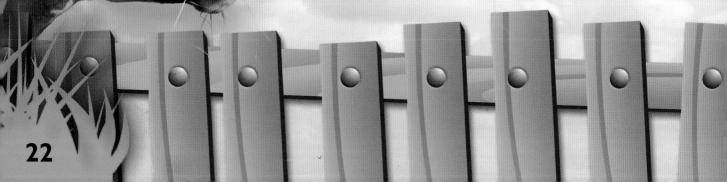

Index

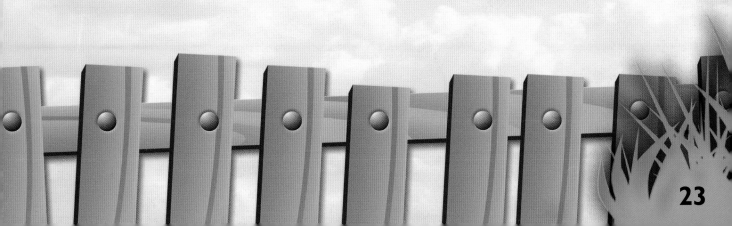

Notes for parents and teachers

Look through the book together, talk about the pictures and find new words in the Glossary.

Talk about the basic needs that animals and humans share, such as food, space, and shelter. Encourage the child to think about how wild animals get their food and find shelter.

It is fun to find ways that animals are similar, or different, to one another—and observing these things is a core science skill. Children could draw pictures of animals with four legs, or ones that eat plants, for example, and go on to identify those that are both plant-eaters and four-legged.

Be prepared for questions about how animals become the meat that we eat. It helps children understand this part of the food chain if they can see it in context: all animals live and die, and farm animals are bred for this purpose.

Cooking together is a great opportunity to have fun and learn. Following a recipe allows children to practice their reading and measuring skills, follow instructions, chat, and be creative. Point out the ways that food changes as ingredients are mixed, heated, or cooled. Talk about eating a balanced diet, and the benefits we receive from the different food groups, including meat, milk, and eggs.